PRAISE FOR SAY GOODBYE TO THE RIVER

With this book, Craig takes us into deep green forests, beside fast silver waters where trout rise, on long hikes over hills flamed by autumn and along slopes of tall, sharp mountains. He takes us into his youth. Everything in the Pacific Northwest of another century comes to life––the people, the animals that make their way along wide or narrow trails, a thriving wilderness of woods and brush and alpine flower. Even the trucks, cabins, fishing gear and rutted roads of a long-gone era fill our imaginations as Craig's rich and evocative writing takes hold. His thoughts, his contemplations and his regrets weave seamlessly in and out of a golden time when the sun shone bright, the rain fell true and the seasons rolled over the shoulders of a young man bursting into life like the leaves on a spring poplar. Think Norman Maclean's *A River Runs Through It*, Ernest Hemingway's *Big Two-Hearted River*, Faulkner's *The Bear* and Sigurd Olson's *The Singing Wilderness.* Nature writing and the writing of the heart at its very best.

— MURRAY PURA AUTHOR OF MAJESTIC AND WILD (BAKER), THE ZOYA SEPTET (MILLERWORDS), A ROAD CALLED LOVE (HARPERCOLLINS)

Even if you aren't a fisherman, Patrick Craig's *Say Goodbye to the River* will make you feel like one (or want to be.) With warmth, insight, humor, and appeals to the five senses, he draws eloquent word pictures of outdoor life and its unquenchable, spiritual allure. His tales made me smile. And yearn.

I look forward to the audio version of these enchanting stories so that I can close my eyes, listen to the poetic language, and be transported into the tranquility and addiction of fishing a high mountain stream. For me, it will be almost as good as being there.

— JEANETTE E. MORRIS AUTHOR, FREELANCE EDITOR, AND AVID FISHERWOMAN

Say Goodbye to the River is a poignant memoir about changes and deep losses. I too am from this precious part of the world called the Pacific Northwest and have seen the destruction of our sacred wilderness. I like how the author resolves this loss in the book and within himself.

— CRYSTAL LYNN • AUTHOR

SAY GOODBYE TO THE RIVER

STORIES FROM THE VANISHING WILDERNESS

PATRICK E. CRAIG

This is a memoir. Names, characters, and places are real but incidents may be used fictitiously.

P&J Publishing PO Box 73, Huston, Idaho 83630

Library of Congress Cataloging—Say Goodbye To The River / Patrick E. Craig

ISBN 978-1-7347635-1-5 (pbk.)

ISBN 978-1-7347635-2-2(eBook)

Printed in the United States of America

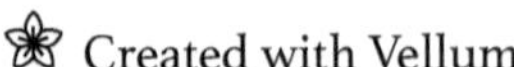

This book is dedicated to the mountains,
and to my uncle, Fred G. Niemi (Knee-me)

ACKNOWLEDGMENTS

Thanks to Murray Pura for his support and friendship in our writing journey.

Thanks to Ernest Hemingway for writing *Big Two-Hearted River* and blazing the trail.

CONTENTS

PROLOGUE

I love the wilderness.

I caught my first trout in Wallowa Lake, Oregon, when I was nine years old. I was staying with my aunt and uncle, Alice and Fred Niemi, who had rented a cabin on the wooded western shore of the lake. The lake itself is four miles long and almost a mile wide, and it sits below the Eagle Cap Wilderness and the Wallowa Range in a huge bowl ground out by some massive antediluvian glacier when the world was fresh. Six miles below the lake is the little town of Joseph, Oregon.

If you travel down the valley, through the Wallowa River Canyon and turn up over the Blue Mountains at Elgin, Oregon, in about an hour you come down into the Walla Walla Valley and the town of Walla Walla, where I grew up.

My aunt and uncle loved that rental cabin so much the next summer they bought their own cabin at the head of the lake. They owned it for thirty-five years. So for me, the towns of Walla Walla and Joseph were the towns I grew up in. My house was in Walla Walla, but I came to life in the mountains around Joseph.

From the window of that rented cabin you could see across the water to the glacial moraine, the ridge that bounds the eastern shore of the lake, its slope unadorned by any trees but alive with the vivid rainbow colors of spring wildflowers. The sun rose from that side in glory, seeking its measured path above the lake to the ridges of Chief Joseph Mountain rising behind the cabin, going up forever into the pristine blue sky, a blue often obscured by the massive thunderheads that rolled in unannounced.

That first morning after we arrived, Uncle Fred woke me up about 5:00 a.m. and told me to get dressed. We had a quick breakfast and then went down to the dock below the cabin and climbed into a small open motorboat. Uncle Fred's friend, Clyde, was waiting with several rods rigged up for trolling. We headed out onto the lake and dropped the lines. I remember it being a cool day, a little overcast. I held my rod, not knowing what to expect. After about fifteen minutes of slowly motoring down the lake, I saw the tip of my pole jerk. Down, up, down, up…

My uncle laughed. "You got one."

"A fish?"

"Yep, a fish. Reel him in."

And so began a lifelong activity that I have never ever tired of—cranking the handle of a fishing reel, be it fly or bait, to drag a feisty, fighting, rainbow trout out of the depths and into the sunlight. There is nothing like it.

But now I am old, and that day was long ago, and over the years since then I have watched the wilderness change. No longer are the mountains a cathedral and we have forgotten the liturgy. It should not be like this.

In these stories I hope to take you back to a time when you could sit on the shore of a lake fishing away the day, and except for the sound of a small motorboat trolling its way down the far side, you could rest in the stillness—but what stillness: the gentle lapping of the waves finding their way down sunlight sparkling diamond paths to the rocky shore, the cry of an osprey circling far above, raptor eyes spying out the hidden paths of the fish in the cool green depths—paths that I only guessed at, the wind moving through the tops of the pine trees with a sound unlike any other I know.

Or the joy of hiking beside a rushing mountain stream, the water pouring down from some unseen glacial snowpack, the eddies and pools alive with pink-sided Rainbows or golden Brookies. Dropping a fly into a small still place under a brushy bank or letting a single egg with a tiny shot weight drift down through the rapids into the flat below and feeling the jerk as the big boy hiding behind the rock gets lured out by the siren call of a Pautzke's Golden Nugget.

Those were the days, fleeting, but foundational to what I am and have become. They won't return, yet in my heart and mind and memories they have a life of their own and will remain, warming my reflections until that day when at last I say goodbye to the river.

1

PAUTZKE'S GOLDEN NUGGETS

They don't make them anymore. That's what I found out when I did a Google search for Pautzke's Golden Nuggets. What are they? Only the best salmon egg trout bait ever made. When I was twelve, if you did not have a couple of jars of Pautzke's in your fishing box, you were far below the rarified heights of genuine angling.

I did a lot of fishing with the magic golden balls up Mill Creek. Mill Creek is an "almost" river that runs right through the middle of Walla Walla, Washington, the town I grew up in. It used to flood every winter so after downtown Walla Walla was almost wiped out in 1931 they built this big, ugly, concrete flood channel that runs from Wildwood Park through the center of town and out to the other side of Rose Street. In the winter when the water is up to the top and raging like Hell's Canyon, it's a death trap. But in the summer you can ride your bike on the slanted floor of the concrete flume all the way through town past the old YMCA and underneath a lot of the buildings in the heart of Walla Walla. Just put your bike down over the short wall by Wildwood Park and you're in.

Outside town to the East, the Army Corps of Engineers built a holding dam and a levee and above that the creek canyon runs east and south way up into the Blue Mountains of Northern Oregon. Every mile of the creek above the dam used to be packed with trout.

I had a twenty-four-inch J.C. Higgins red and black fat-tired bike that I earned the money for by mowing my grandpa's lawn. I spent the summer before I was in the third grade doing that job and made twenty dollars. My dad chipped in the other twenty and we went right down to Sears and bought that beauty. I rode that bike until I graduated from high school. Coaster brakes and handlebars with a holder for a flashlight; it was a hummer. I could hang my trombone over the right handlebar when I went to band practice, but more importantly, I could hang my fishing rod there too.

IT'S A SUMMER DAY AND I START EARLY. IT'S ABOUT thirteen miles up to Kooskooskie, a wide spot in the road going over the top of the Blues. Head out east on Isaacs Street and then turn up Mill Creek Road. Paved for part of the way, the road becomes dusty gravel about five miles out. I can keep going as far as I want. But today about six miles up I pull off the road, find an open place that doesn't have a cabin on it, and get down to the creek.

I've got my rod, my Eagle Claw #10 snelled hooks, the ones with the eagle diving from the red top of the packet and the fisherman with a fish on—the real deal in fishhooks. A canvas trout bag slung over my shoulder with a plastic tube of small split-shot lead weights and a jar of Golden Nuggets shoved in the pocket of my denim shorts. There's a paper bag in the basket on the back of the bike with a peanut butter sandwich wrapped in waxed paper. I am good to go.

My rod is short, so I won't get the tip tangled in the bushes. No leader, line tied to the loop in the four-inch piece of line snelled to the hook and a tiny lead weight about two feet up the line, bitten down on to make it stay where I want it.

I put a Golden Nugget on the hook, being careful to make sure the barb and the shank disappear inside the egg. The Eagle Claw single-egg hook is gold so the trout can't see it unless you let it poke out of the egg. I walk along the bank looking for a riffle—one that races down over some rocks and then drops into a deeper stretch. The big boys hang out in the hole at the bottom of the run, waiting for caddis or grasshoppers that have fallen into the creek. I drop in my line.

The water carries the little lead weight, dragging it down through the rocks and then that golden egg drops into the pool. If they are going to go after the bait, it will be now. And it is.

The fish hits the egg and turns to run, but my line pulls him up short. Whoosh! Out of the water he comes, twelve inches and fat. He's been hiding in that hole a while. Maybe he never got tricked by a Golden Nugget before. Out he comes again, and I work him to the bank. He's a fighter, and he tries to make one more run out into the creek. The pole bends and he flops, churning the water, trying to spit that hook. No good. Now he's out on the bank and thrashing in the tall grass, leaping and jerking. I grab him and he squirts out of my hand, desperate. No, I got him this time. I crack his back on a rock and he goes limp. One more crack and he's done.

I open his mouth to retrieve the hook. The line disappears down his throat. He swallowed everything. I pull and the hook comes out, bringing some of him with it. Into the bag he goes, and I walk on down the creek.

It's a hot summer day, like many in my hometown. The clinging, musty smell of the water weeds along the bank mixes with the sweet scent of fresh hay, cut and laying in bales scattered in the field behind me. Out on the road a pea-viner rumbles, a cloud of dust following like a monstrous dirty brown ghost. He's headed up to the Ferrell place for the late harvest. I see some girls on horseback, but they are not looking for a twelve-year-old kid that smells of fish.

I follow the creek. Sometimes I wonder where it goes after it runs through town. Like when I left Walla Walla the first time. I traveled by car with my family down to Portland, and just outside of town we drove past The Last Chance Gas Station and Café. Looking out the rear window, I had the oddest feeling I would never see my town again and this was my last chance to stop, to get out of the car and go back. Like the sign really meant it. If I went past this point, I would never make it home again.

I have thought of that moment often over the years and wondered why I ever left, why I went outside the circle of everything I knew and went from here to there, but never back again. And here, at the end of my ride, I know that everything I ever needed was right there, right in my town, and I could have lived there all my life, and found a girl and gotten married and taught English and writing in the local high school and played at the M&F Supper Club in Milton-Freewater on weekends and I could have ridden my bike up Mill Creek with a pocket full of Pautzke's Golden Nuggets any summer day and never wondered about the world outside. And been happy and lived in a house looking up at the Blue Mountains like my great grandfather and my grandfather, and my uncle. And it would have been enough.

But I didn't. And that's sad—because those days are like Pautzke's Golden Nuggets. They don't make them anymore.

2

THE CANYON

I love waking up in my uncle's house. They always give me the room at the end of the hallway. I sleep in the bed against the right-hand wall. There is one on the other side of the room, but I never sleep in it.

I keep the window open a crack for fresh air in the night. There's a bird singing outside, and that's what wakens me. It's one of those quiet Walla Walla mornings, sun just stirring the town from slumber, soft rays of light filtering through the birch trees lining the parking in front of the house. I can see them outside the window, their white trunks like sentinels guarding my dreams.

My Uncle Fred is a CPA. He manages estates for the rich ranchers and does taxes for the business men that are the elite in Walla Walla. I've heard that he never misplaced one dime in his work, nor has he ever done a dishonest or even questionable accounting trick to help his clients. My uncle is Finnish, his family came to America at the turn of the twentieth century, and he has old world values.

I never hear him really swear except once. A client calls him and asks him to do something shady. Not illegal, but questionable. I hear it from the other room, her voice tinny and whining on the phone. He is quiet while she talks, then he shouts into the phone.

"Dammit, Ginger, you got a hell of a nerve asking me to do that. Find yourself another CPA." Only he didn't just say, "dammit." The phone slams down. He walks into the kitchen, pours a half tumbler of vodka from a bottle in the cupboard and downs it in three gulps. The phone rings again. It's her, a disconnected voice on the other end. I can hear the desperation. She begs him to take her back. I can almost see her groveling on her knees. He shows mercy, but not without a caveat. "If you ever ask me to do anything even slightly shady ever again, we are done, and I mean it." She thanks him. "Yes, Fred" and "Thank you, Fred," over and over. He hangs up.

My uncle is ruthlessly honest, a dry sense of humor, not a romantic. He's also a deacon at the Episcopal Church. On Sundays he carries the golden offering plate up to the altar. He never tells me he loves me—not in words, anyway. I just know by the way he teaches me, includes me in his life, makes things happen for me.

WE TAKE OFF AROUND FIVE IN THE MORNING, JUST MY uncle and me. We leave the house on Clinton Street, my aunt still asleep in the bedroom off the kitchen. He's driving his light blue '56 Chevy Nomad station wagon. It's his pride and joy. The Pflueger rods, also my uncle's pride and joy, are stashed in the back with the waders, the red tackle bag with the Pflueger Medalist reels and the blue cooler. We're headed for the canyon.

Down the road to Milton-Freewater, across the state line, not a lot of traffic. A few wheat trucks rumble by—it's July, harvest time, and the town has come alive. All the teachers at the local schools are off for the summer, driving wheat trucks in the fields or forklifts at the elevators and the canneries. Walla Walla is farm country and wheat is the lifeblood.

Midway between Milton and Athena is the Tollgate turnoff. A big swinging left turn, and up the hill. When we get to the top, the entire valley spreads out like a chessboard, tan expanses of ripe wheat rolling away to the North and West. The heads of the wheat bow down, waiting for the grinding John Deere harvesters to bring them in—believers gathered to their savior, who comes with a scythe and a fan in his hand.

Off in the haze the dormant volcanoes—Adams, Jefferson, St. Helens—march north, their perfect cones a reminder that fire and smoke can hide just beneath the surface of all beauty.

Up into the Blue Mountains, the road winding between tall stands of pine crammed together, shoulder to shoulder, Braddock's soldiers marching into the French trap. Past Tollgate, Spout Springs, Langdon Lake, and down the hill to Elgin. We come into town past the logging mill with stacks of huge pine logs piled up, sprinklers on top keeping them wet so they won't split before they get sawed into boards. The rusty teepee burner belches smoke through the screened top, burning the sawdust and waste. The smell of the pine touches everything in Elgin; the people live because of the smell of the pine.

Turn left at the stop sign, but you don't have to wait if nobody's coming, jog right, past the little gas station then the long hill up to the top and start down the Minam Grade. My uncle says back in the thirties it took all day to get down this hill, but now the Nomad screams around the corners and we hit bottom going eighty. "Nothing wrong with speed if you control it." My uncle grins, his gold bridgework glinting. The little town of Minam, the yellow highway sign that says "Rattlesnake Crossing" and shows snakes on the road. The Minam River flows into the Wallowa here, and we cross the long bridge and head south down the canyon.

Below us the river winds through the trees, disappears, reappears, the surface cracked diamonds in the sun as the road hums against the tires. We come to the pullout. Around the corner, the sagging wooden bridge spans the river. The old house sits above, staring down the canyon toward the mountains as it has every day I've fished here.

Waders, fishing vests, the Pflueger rods and reels, creel—make sure I have the round red tin of Mucilin and my net, we're good. One last check for the small box of Niemi Specials. Yellow, like a hornet, with a black head, red thread and buck-tail-brown wings, it's the only fly we use. My uncle heads upstream, I go down. "See you later," he says. He's not afraid to leave me alone on the river, and I lift my thirteen-year-old shoulders to look taller.

I edge down the bank into the river, silent and green, not too high. Across, on the far bank, the bushes crowd over, almost touch the surface. The hills lift above the trees, some bare, the red rock outcroppings splashes of blood against the brown grass. A dippy bird on a rock, up and down, then plunging in after a caddis. The railroad follows the river across the way. If you can get across, you can walk clear back to La Grande on the tracks.

First cast into the flat in front of the bushes. A small

trout rises, looks at the fly as it bobs by then flashes away. Again, closer to the bank. This time a bigger one rushes out and snaps the fly up. Away with a rush, the rod bending a bit, but not a two pounder. I lift the tip and he hits the end of the line. A flash of silver in the sunlight and then he's coming, fighting against the clicking of the reel, the green line bringing him inexorably in. I dip him out with the net and wade against the pull of the water, back to the bank.

He's flipping in the net, the fly a deadly boutonniere on his jutting lower jaw. Small, nine inches maybe, but a keeper. I wet my hand and take him, a quick blow against a rock and he is still in my hand, one more to make sure.

I unhook the fly. It's matted with blood and mucus, so I smear it with Mucilin and blow on it to fluff the wings. The sun is up over the rim of the canyon now. I wonder if death will take us all like that, the hand of God reaching down and cracking our back against a rock. But this is not a death day, it's life and nothing but the river, and the sun on the water like a thousand candles and the warm air moving in the trees and the voice of the river speaks to my soul.

My wader has a leak and I can feel the slow coolness of the water as it creeps into the boot. I move down the river casting, the fly arcing over my head, following where the pole points. Don't stay too long in one place, if they don't take it in the first few casts they are not interested.

Hours fly by unnoticed. It's just me, the river, the cool water, the sun on my back, the fish in my creel. The sun moves west, now it's dipping behind the canyon wall. Have we been here all day?

Above me on the road, a blue Suburban rolls by. The horn honks. It's my aunt, heading for the cabin at the head of the lake. Time to go. Wade across the river and climb out. My foot makes a squishing noise as I walk back down the road. Around the corner, there's the car, my uncle already stripping off his waders.

"Get any?"

I show him the five trout in my creel. He grins. "Good, good."

I sit on the tailgate and pull my waders off. The water pours out.

"Leak, huh? I'll fix it tonight." Another patch on the waders, like a badge of honor. I shiver in the cool dusk. My uncle reaches in his red bag and pulls out a silver flask. He grins again. "Blue Mountain Mule Kick. This will warm you up." And it is, and it does.

We follow the road. The canyon lets us go, the valley opens ahead, the mountains rising from the green fields, the snow touching the tops. But behind me, the canyon is always there, waiting, speaking to me in a voice that only those who love the river will ever hear.

3

THE BLUE HOLE

He turned left into the Indian Crossing Campground, the gravel creaking under the wheels of his car. The drive from Joseph up over Salt Creek Summit had been dreary, burned out trees from the Lick Creek Fire still stood, ominous, dead, black, the new growth spreading a green carpet among the silent snags. The old logger at the restaurant in town told him that the armchair environmentalists over in Portland wouldn't let them cut burned trees, so he and his friends sat day after day without a job, nursing their coffee and a big grudge.

"Millions of board feet, rotting. They could build all the damn affordable housing they want. Idiots."

The old man went back to his coffee. No answers in the black cup.

He paid his bill and as he left, the waitress called him "Hon." Down Main Street, past the sign.

> "This little town is heaven to us, don't drive like hell through it."

Outside of Joseph, the prairie ran flat to the base of Mount Howard and the moraine. Straight ahead was Hell's Canyon and across the Snake, the Seven Devils of Idaho. He turned right on Wallowa Mountain Road. There were ranches set back off the road, then the new pavement ended and he was in the forest, the way marred with potholes and curves. He smoked a cigarette, stubbed it out in the ashtray.

A mountain brook poured down the hill at a wide sweeping turn, more like a waterfall than a stream. Thirty miles to Blackhorse campground, then Ollokot. He pulled to a stop. At the junction, the sign pointed left to Halfway or right up the gravel road to Indian Crossing. He turned right.

The campground was overgrown with weeds and brush. A few one-man tents poked their heads above the vine maple and snow bush that clogged the once pristine grounds. A single hand-pumped water wheel stood at the entrance of the parking area, the only reminder that once these mountains had been a well-maintained paradise for campers and hikers with plenty of faucets and toilets and electricity coming off a pole to power the pump for the well.

Fifty feet away, a man crawled out of a tent . He was dirty with a ragged beard. It looked like he was a fixture. Around his site were scattered the flotsam and jetsam of a person who had no idea what the mountains were about. A battered white Ford Pinto was parked in the campsite.

The fisherman turned away, shook his head.

Didn't use to be like this.

HE REMEMBERED COMING WITH HIS UNCLE AND COUSIN, years before, filling their bottles from the water tap—turning on the faucet and getting cold, clean, mountain water, then heading for the Blue Hole, two miles up the canyon. The day had been hot. They wore t-shirts, fishing jackets and long pants.

"Keeps the rattlesnakes off your legs," his uncle had said.

The sun above them divided the north and south walls of the canyon like a compass, and the river spoke to them as they walked. They kept their rods pointed ahead so they wouldn't catch in the brush along the trail. He had snapped a tip off once. His uncle hadn't said a word, but the look on his face was educational.

A big yellow grasshopper flew across the trail and

landed. He reached down slowly and picked it off the log. It stared up at him, a black blob of tobacco juice oozing from its jaws.

"Gonna go bait fishing?"

The question floated, a barb in the air, and he looked at his cousin who grinned.

He shook his head.

"Nope, just looking."

He threw the hopper. It took flight and winged away, the buzz of its wings cards on bike spokes.

The Niemi Specials in his jacket were enough for that day.

They followed the river. The trail soft, easy going for a kid. July, the river down, the rocks making white breaks in the current, the smooth places dark with the green water rippling over the stony bottom. Small rocks worn smooth by the pounding high water of spring, carried down from Eagle Cap.

Clouds rolled in, but not rain. Bursts of white followed them up the river. The trail took them higher, into the tall pines and away from the soft murmur, but they knew the river was still there.

Two miles, the trail split. They followed the left fork, the sign that said Twin Lakes — Blue Hole. The trail came back down to the Imnaha. They could cross here and go to Twin Lakes or follow the right-hand bank. They went right. Just above the crossing was the Blue Hole.

The sidewalls of the canyon which had soared off into the puffy white on blue as they walked up from Indian Crossing closed in on them, only fifty feet wide, squeezing the river into a deep crevasse.

"We could go to the other Blue Hole, but that's three miles up some rough trail. We'll try here a bit, but the lunkers are crafty," his uncle said. "They've seen every fly made, so it's an iffy proposition."

He'd taken his place at the head of the pool, Mike in the middle, his uncle at the bottom where the smooth water broke into pieces and ran down mossy rocks. The ritual—check the fly, tippet, leader, the green line through every guide. The sun was hot on his back; he could feel the sweat under his arms. Back with the rod, forward, back again, pulling the green line out of the reel, feeling the weight of it as it hissed through the guides. The fly at the end fluffed, looking like a grasshopper, out to the edge of the pool where the river roiled down over the rocks and spread like molasses in the shadow of the walls.

The fly settled on smooth, deep water. A small trout rushed at it, but he pulled the fly away and put it back a few feet to the right, toward the darkness where the deep water was.

He saw the fish before it hit the fly. It came up from under the rock wall, moving like a torpedo, big and hungry. The trout didn't waste time jumping; he just rushed his nose above the surface, took the fly and ran for the bottom.

He pulled the tip up, but it didn't stop the trout. The clicking of the reel feeding line broke the stillness. He got it stopped before it slipped behind the rock and led it out. The fight was not on the surface like it would be with an eight-incher. This trout ran back and forth across the bottom, fighting the crank of the reel and looking for an escape route. He lifted again, the pole bending under the great weight of the lovely big fish.

"Whooeee, you got one," his cousin shouted. His uncle looked up. They both put down their rods and came to watch.

Now the trout headed toward the surface and then out he came, flipping his head to spit the fly. He could see he had hooked it from the outside and snagged it under the jaw. No way that fly was coming off. Back in with a splash, the water pushed away and then collapsing back into the hole the trout left in the surface. The big fish went down again, looking for a sharp edge to cut the line, or a snag to wrap around, but he held it up and led it toward the shore. A few more minutes and he landed it, flopping in a small pool between the rocks, gills pumping, fighting for breath.

He laid his pole down and reached into the water with both hands, feeling the glacier cold river run through his fingers. Then he took hold of the trout, touching the skin with wet hands so he wouldn't take off the protective slime, hooked a finger under the gills, lifted it up. His cousin and his uncle nodded. Then he gave a jerk on the fly and pulled it from under the jaw. The fish flipped its tail, looking up at him with popped eyes. He looked up at his uncle.

"Yep, let him swim, he's too big for the pan, anyway."

He set the fish down in the water. It stayed for a minute in the shallows by the edge, gills pumping oxygen back into its body. Then in a flash it was gone, headed for the deep pocket on the other side of the river.

His cousin grinned. "He won't come out of there for a while."

They fished the pool a while longer, offering flies for lunch, but the commotion had closed the restaurant. After a while, they headed back downstream, fishing as they went.

BUT THAT WAS THEN, AND THIS WAS NOW. HE REMEMBERED the big trout. He wondered if it had lived on in the pool, or if some tinhorn in a clean vest with a Walmart rod had pulled him out, dumped him in the bushes to draw the bears, then headed back to his apartment in Portland.

He left his car locked tight with the alarm on. He didn't trust the bearded guy. He took his rod and jacket and headed up the trail. The sun didn't warm him today like it had back then. The trail was dustier, and when he got to the fork in the trail, another fire had burned down the cathedral pines and he could see the river flowing through burnt dirt with small patches of green struggling through the ash.

When he came to the Blue Hole, he saw the sign.

> *Oregon no longer plants non-native trout in this section of the Imnaha. We have done this to encourage the return of salmon to the upper portion of the river. Please do not disturb the gravel spawning beds when walking in the water.*

He read the sign again and spit into the bushes. He lit another cigarette and got his rod ready, tied on a fly and went to the head of the pool. He cast out and watched the fly as it moved slowly toward the end of the pool. His eye caught the glint of something silver hanging in the bottom of the pool. He cast again, and the silver moved toward the fly.

Salmon?

The fish jerked the fly and tried to run. But it was sluggish and weak. He reeled it in and pulled it out of the water. A grey fish with yellow fins and an ugly sucking mouth flopped at the water's edge.

Squawfish!

He picked up the sucker with dry hands and beat its head against a rock. The fish spit blood and then stopped moving. He pulled the fly out of its mouth and then threw it as far as he could into the woods.

You don't even belong in this river dead.

He thought of the big trout again. His uncle was gone, but he would call his cousin when he got back to the motel and ask him if he remembered the trout. He knew what Mike would say. He would tell him that he remembered. It was good that someone did.

4

THE CABIN

My aunt and uncle's cabin is at the end of the Wallowa Lake Highway. At least it says that on the maps, but we know it is Powerhouse Road because of the generator driven by the creek that comes from the dam up the Aneroid trail. The tin shed sits off the road at the base of the trail that marks the end of traffic, the gateway into the heart of the Eagle Cap Wilderness. Pack it in, pack it out. The water comes roaring out and the power lights all the cabins at this end of the lake.

We drive up from Joseph, down the east side of the lake, and when we come around by the old Wallowa Lake Lodge, we turn left. Past the mini golf and Flying Arrow resort, past Valli's Swiss restaurant where Maggie Valli serves homemade rolls and my uncle takes two out of the basket and puts them in his pocket for later. A quarter mile past the Wallowa Lake Pack Station and we come to the cabin. Out front there is a mailbox with their name, Niemi. Below that, my uncle writes, "Knee-me" so strangers will know how to pronounce it.

They buy the cabin when I am nine years old. I'm with my aunt when she drives up from Walla Walla to look at it. They own it two weeks later, so I always think of it as my cabin. Before they buy it they rent places at the lake, but they want something of their own. They pay twelve thousand dollars for it. It is a classic old wooden cabin on an acre, simple, two bedrooms, one bathroom with a metal stall shower. All knotty pine inside and a deck that sits right above Aneroid Creek. Wrap-around picture windows in the back. My aunt looks across the creek at the empty acre with the beautiful tall pines over there and when it comes up for sale, they buy it so they won't have to worry about another cabin going in and ruining their view.

I am there often over the next thirty-five years. It is fishing central. We come up from a day in the canyon and my uncle patches waders and sets them in front of the roaring fire while my aunt fries trout. At dinner, I ask her why she never eats many trout, and she smiles.

"I've been cooking trout since 1933 and I've eaten hundreds. I've had my share, you just eat up."

Eating trout is easy. If you cleaned it right there are no

gills and no side fins. Grab the head, stick your fork in the side under the head and peel the hot white or pink meat from the bones. If it's cooked well, each side comes right off in one piece. I eat my fill. Nothing like trout right out of the river. The bone plate piled with fish heads, skeletons and tails. You can keep your catfish, bluegills, smallmouth bass. At the cabin, those aren't even fish.

I split a lot of wood in the back yard and stack it in the small tool shed off the deck. Pine and fir to feed the fireplace. I help my uncle build a horseshoe pit in the front yard and we pitch horseshoes for hours.

Some days we go back down to the foot of the lake and park by the Old Chief Joseph monument. We head across the small, well kept lawn that surrounds the cairn, go down a trail to the dam at the end of the lake, walk across the spillway and climb down to the lower Wallowa River. Down in the dark canyon is a lot of good fishing. As we walk across, water from the lake pours down a mossy wooden spillway into a pool below. The sign says, "No sliding" but local kids slide down the mossy wooden sluice anyway. Many a kid goes home with a big wooden splinter in their butt.

The last picture I have with my uncle is of him, my brother, and me. We are in front of the monument. His thick black glasses sit crooked on his face. In his sixties they found a melanoma on his ear, so they sliced off the top half. After that he calls himself "Ol' One Ear," and he has to balance his glasses on the stump or they slip down on that side.

The cabin is a place of shelter for me. Home life is uncertain, my mom is sick, my dad gone a lot. My aunt and uncle open a world of wonder and rest for me. Only members of the upper crust own a cabin at Wallowa Lake, and that gives me a certain cachet among my peers. When I leave the demands of home and head for the mountains, I know that life will stay on an even keel for at least a little while.

The days don't have edges at the cabin, they flow from one to another and then you go home. A bright sunny day turns into a huge bone-rattling thunderstorm and then clears to white puffs of clouds. The mountains don't know what time it is. Across the road, the Episcopal day camp celebrates their outdoor Sunday services. Does the pastor know they are in God's cathedral?

Beyond the outdoor chapel are the falls of the Wallowa and the Boy Scout Camp. In the spring I walk through the fragrant pines and watch the Kokanee, bright red, spawning and dying in the Wallowa River. Hot summer days. Take a spinning rod and walk up the upper Wallowa trail with a jar of Pautzke's Golden Nuggets or a big plastic marshmallow bait jar filled with grasshoppers I catch along the way.

When my uncle first comes here in the thirties, the rivers are alive with trout. No limits. You catch a hundred trout in a day. Take the panners; leave the big boys to keep the streams filled. He makes light of bait fishing, but it is my uncle who takes me way down the east side of the lake to a place where a big pine rises and the shoreline makes a little jut out into the lake.

"An old Indian showed me," he says, and I want to meet that fellow because down below that pine, all the big trout swim by. You put a three-foot leader with a swivel on your line, but not before you slip a medium sliding weight on above. A white marshmallow, a worm, and cast way out into the dark depths, the weight swinging the line down into the feeding zone, and the worm wiggling on the end, floating, the white spot in the dark catching the eye of the hungry trout. I catch trout there all day.

The bed in my room is always soft, the walls have Audubon prints of quail and ducks, the oil heater has a pipe with a decorative circular cover surrounding it where it goes into the wall, so you don't see the rough edges of the pine boards where the guy who built it cut the hole with a jigsaw. In the kitchen, a tiny gas stove, the old Amana fridge with a metal icebox with ice trays in it. A radio sits on the windowsill and my aunt plays country and western music from the local radio station in Joseph every morning. The lamps in the front room are from the thirties with translucent shades that let the light through. Their light is soft and the old couch pulls me in, a friend.

The green and red cover has pictures of horses and barns. In the corner is my uncle's chair. I don't sit there unless he is not at the cabin, and then I try it out, feeling the spot where the cushion surrendered and smelling his after-shave. I bring Zane Grey books to read and leave them there for the next trip. The cat sits in the window watching the chipmunks outside, chattering his teeth against the glass.

I AM THIRTY-EIGHT WHEN MY UNCLE DIES, AND WHEN I GET the news, I cry like a baby. My aunt keeps the cabin for a few more years. Then without telling me, she sells it to a guy named Cactus Jack, a local celebrity who owns a bar in Joseph. He has it for three years. When I drive by, I see his trailer parked where the horseshoe pit used to be, the windows of the cabin unwashed and the gutters filled with pine needles. It looks alone and I want to walk up to the old screen door to comfort it, tell it that everything is all right, that I will come back as soon as I catch my limit.

When he goes bankrupt, Cactus Jack defaults on the loan and my aunt takes it back. She offers it to me for $80,000 but I'm broke and that number might as well be a million. So she sells it to a lady from Portland who remodels it into a no-character house, and the cabin is gone. "Knee me" is replaced by a big rock with a square metal plate that has their name on it as though Custer is buried there.

Now that end of the lake is a tourist trap with three mini-golfs, a go-kart track, ice cream stores. People from California try to find a signal on their cellphones, the trailhead is packed with cars filled with people who read about the wilderness in a magazine.

I still go there, I drive by, but the new modern house pushes away the drifts of memory. All things change, but I wish some didn't.

Sometimes I wonder if heaven has cabins and if it does, is my cabin still there? Will I get to drive up from Walla Walla, past the lake, and turn at "Knee-me" into the soft pine needle driveway between the tall trees? Will the sound of the creek still my heart, and the fire blazing in the hearth comfort me? I hope so.

I want heaven to be familiar.

metal plate that has the name of a cottage [illegible] is nailed there.

Now the end of the lake is dotted with [illegible] mansions for [illegible] from California [illegible] about the [illegible] The [illegible] is [illegible] with [illegible] filled with people who [illegible] about the [illegible] in magazines.

I still go there. I drive by [illegible] modern houses [illegible] of memory. All [illegible] like I did?

Sometimes I wonder if [illegible] cabin still [illegible] from Walla Walla past the lake and turn [illegible] the [illegible] drive [illegible] the sound of [illegible] on the [illegible] I hope so.

[illegible] there.

5

WALTER BRENNAN

He hadn't been to the Indian Lodge Motel in years. The brown shingle roof was gone, replaced by red tiles. It didn't say Walter Brennan's Indian Lodge on the sign. Brennan had been dead a long time—since 1974.

He remembered Chief Joseph Days. Brennan, the Grand Marshall of the parade, waving from the back seat of a red Lincoln convertible. The crowd of locals cheering. No bronze foundry yet, no tourists, no artsy-fartsys with their city politics and "let's change all this" ideas. His aunt beside him, watching the horses, taking pictures with her Rolleiflex.

Back then, no spotted owls, plenty of jobs for lumberjacks and farmers, no marijuana store where the restaurant used to be. Chief Joseph days—cute girls with long hair tied back in ponytails, the wind whipping them out as they flew around the arena with sponsor flags gripped in their hands, horses stretched out and running low to the ground. Or dressed in fringed outfits prancing palomino horses down the main street, no one minding the droppings because they smelled like home.

He grabbed his suitcase out of the back seat of the van and went in to register. The clerk looked him over, a pimple-faced girl with purple hair and an ugly tattoo on her arm, a bug in a box. She asked for ID and his license plate number.

"I used to come here when I was a kid. Walter Brennan owned it."

"Who?"

"Walter Brennan. You're not from around here?"

"No."

He didn't like her. She had no idea what this place was about.

"You know, when I was a kid you only saw tattoos on military guys and jailbirds."

"What?"

She looked at him. The words hadn't registered. He grinned. He held out his hand, and she gave him the key. "One fourteen. Checkout's at 11:00." She picked up her iPhone and started texting.

He went to his room and put his bag on the bed. He stripped down and went in the bathroom. The showers were new, not the old white metal frame boxes he remembered. Nicer, but not the same.

He showered a long time, the water hot and clean, washing away the years, the distance. He dried off, put on jeans, a t-shirt, his wallet and Swiss Army knife in his pants pocket. The clock read 12:00. Mid-day, but you never knew when trout would bite. He locked the room and walked across the lot to the van. He could see pimple face at the desk, still texting, a purple lock in her hair drooping down over a vacuous face. The sun glinted off the glass, and she disappeared, gone from his mind and his thoughts, gone like a cool breeze.

He pulled out his rod. Not the Pflueger, that was treasure. He got out the rod he'd bought at Fred Meyers in Nampa. Nice, but nothing in it, no memories, no pictures, not like the rod in the silver case. This one didn't carry the years like a mantle, the miles and hot sun on his back and days on the river.

It was too late to go back to the canyon, so he drove out of town toward the lake. When he came to the monument, he parked under the big pines. He pulled out his rod and put on his fishing jacket. Remembered when his uncle, dying from the leukemia, had given it to him. He didn't say, "I love you," he just handed him the jacket. But there was something in his eye, and as he looked at his uncle he knew. Knew about the years, and the trout, and the lessons and the life poured into him.

Check for flies, Mucilin, Oregon fishing license. He walked across the grass by the monument, but the trail stopped at a fence. He went down to the left toward the lake, but the fence ran all the way to the beach. He walked around toward the dam, but it was fenced all along the grassy hillside. When he came to the spillway, there was a sign. "Private property, no trespassing."

The path to the spillway went on past the fence, but it was filled with weeds, not walked on, disheveled. The trees had overgrown the canyon below the dam and it was dark, no sun, and he couldn't see the river.

What the hell is this?

No way over. He went back. He got into the van and did a U-turn onto the road. There was some kind of Indian visitor center with roadside signs. He drove past, into town, took a left and went around to the lower end of the canyon. Down the street to the place where the river flowed out of the trees into Joseph. Another fence, another sign. "Private Property. Use restricted. Please contact..." and an address in town where he could get written permission to visit *his* river.

I'm glad he isn't here.

He looked through the fence, but it was overgrown with weeds and brush here too, and he couldn't see the river. The pool was not far, where his uncle showed him the roll cast, beyond that the trail along the silver sliding water, where you stood and cast over to the little shallow riffles on the far side, drawing trout out of their hiding places. The gate on the fence was rusty, the lock had a spider web. No one came here.

He walked back to his van, the dust puffing under his tennis shoes, clinging to his jeans. He drove through town and headed for Enterprise. Five miles. Past Prairie Creek. He had never fished there, he always wondered if there were trout.

When he got to Enterprise, he made the left turn toward Safeway and stopped in front of the Mexican restaurant. An old house. Used to be a family here, but now painted salmon and green with a green fence out front and a sign. He sat down outside at a table on the porch and the woman who smiles came out. Chips, salsa, Margarita. The lime was cool, the salt bit. He drank it fast —ordered another. Fajitas. Another Margarita.

When he finished, he paid cash and went back to the car. The tequila kept his head from flashing pictures.

He wondered if he could drive all the way back.

6

THE LAKE

He never brought girls to this spot, but he brought her. He had waited a long time for a girl who loved to fish, who knew what it meant. She was from Idaho, her dad was a hunter, she had her own tent when he met her—and camping gear. It was icing on the cake.

A narrow pull-off by a guardrail on the Wallowa Lake Highway. The tall pine tree his uncle showed him, the rocky "almost a trail" down to the beach. The sun hot on the lake, waves from passing boats and a little breeze.

The descent is steep but they are still young, they slide the last few feet, laughing. There are big rocks here, rip-rap below the dirt bank to keep the road from sliding. They climb down through them. It was a dry spring, not much rain. The lake is low, below the boulders, and the beach is there, sand, pebbles, a piece of leader that someone cut off. A red bobber under a root. The little spit of land sticking out into the lake.

He looked around for some dead branches. Cut the forks out of them and stuck the 'y's into the sand. He had set the rods up already. Long casters with Daiwa reels, a three-foot leader with a swivel, a medium sliding lead weight above it. Number 12 hook, black against the white marshmallow. The round white box of worms from the gas station in Wallowa. Pull out a big one, cut it in half with the Swiss Army knife. Put them on the hooks, the worms wiggling, practicing their siren call. Rigged up, good to go.

He released the bail on the first rod, held the line against the rod with his finger, swung the rod back and cast. The weight pulled the line off the reel, singing through the guides, out to the waiting water. The weight hit, a brief splash, and it sinks, still pulling the line off. He doesn't close the bail until it stops, the line still holding the shape of the reel in a long twirl, the breeze pulling the line into a curve. After a few minutes he flipped the bail and reeled in, watching the curls come out of the line, feeling the weight grabbing the sandy bottom, then hanging. The line tightens, and the rod tip bends down. He set it in the 'y' and pushed the butt of the rod down into the sand. He looked at her.

"Good to go. Watch the tip."

"I know." She smiles.

He takes his rod, casts twenty feet to the right, same distance out. Sets it in the other 'y' and sits beside her.

The sun glitters on the lake, shards of broken glass ruffled by the breeze blowing out toward town. Across the water, the cabins and homes on the west side are visible through the trees. He can see the Harris place and points it out to her. Further down is the huge mansion. A local who went bankrupt built it. There is a boathouse at the top of the slope and a slider ramp to lower boats into the lake. A huge dock, two decks, a balcony. He's seen pictures of the inside because it's for sale for a million and a half. Bucket list stuff.

Offshore from them is a swimming platform. You can rent them at the Marina, some are private, but today this one is empty.

They wait. He looks at her. She's settled, peaceful, the lake has done its magic. They talk in low voices about everything and nothing. One hundred yards offshore a boat slips by, the Evinrude set to low speed. The lines are out on both sides, the trolling rigs looking for Mackinaw or Kokanee. The motor throbs, they are drinking beer. He can't tell what brand, but it's a great idea. The boat passes and the wake comes in a "vee" straight at them, then breaks with a rush at their feet. The sound frightens the stillness, then it settles again. He puts his arm around her and kisses her. She likes it.

She points at his rod.

"Got one."

The tip is pulsing, down, up, down. He grabs the rod and pulls up and back. Got him! The reel is silent but strong, pulling the trout up to the sun, out of the dark water. Ten yards out, the trout breaks the surface. A flash then down again but the pole holds him and brings him back. Closer. Another flash, then he's landed. The trout flops on the wet sand right at the edge of the water, rainbows and molten silver. He picks it up, the eyes facing him, and cracks its back on a rock. Again. The blood on the mouth shows red against the silver skin. It twitches once more, then lies still in his hand. Without taking the hook out, he rinses it off in the lake. The trout has swallowed the bait, so he pulls until the internals give and the hook comes out. He runs the red stringer through the gills, puts one end under a rock, and sets the fish in the water to stay cool. He sets another bait, marshmallow, worm, and casts it out. He washes his hands in the water, the slime and scales twinkling in the shallows.

They sit for a long time. He feels her near him, her body and her presence. A thought crosses his mind, but he's awkward and there are boats and water skiers, so he lets the idea slip away.

The sun is easing toward the top of Chief Joseph Mountain across the lake, and the breeze dies to nothing. A great peace settles. The dancing diamonds smooth to green ice, the only sound is the rustling of the tiny waves coming in. The lake is absolutely still and smooth and he can see the shoreline, the mountain, a perfect mirror image on the far side.

Nothing moves. It is as though the day is holding its breath. The sun slides behind the ridge, more, each piece disappearing into a split in time, into the place where tomorrow lives. The last ray pierces the oranges, the deep pinks, the growing blue. One last rim of light and then it goes. A tiny breeze springs up and the surface of the lake splinters into a million pieces.

Now! Both tips go down at the same time. They laugh and grab their poles. They catch fish for another hour, one after another. It is a good day.

HE STANDS LOOKING DOWN AT THE PLACE WHERE THEY fished that day. Out at the platform, two boats are tied up. Young people are drinking beer and the sound of their music is bloody talons in the air. He swings his legs over the guardrail and walks to the edge. The trail has eroded, cracks where the stepping rocks have washed out. The lake is high and there is no beach. The lines would tangle in the rocks.

Besides, he's too old to get down.

7

JAWS

The trout was big, the biggest he ever caught in the canyon.

He had been on the river all afternoon. It was fall, and the river was low. The grass was waist high and brown along the banks. Tamarack and aspen lent their gold and red to the September kaleidoscope that covered the hills. The afternoon brought a chill wind, warning of the coming snow that already mantled the lofty peaks. The sun was just going down over the western wall of the canyon when he came to the fallen tree. And that's when he caught it.

He was staying at the cabin by himself. He had arrived late the night before and used the key hidden under the pine stump by the kitchen window to get in. It smelled the same. Faint hint of fried trout mixed with the bayberry candles his aunt lit on the mantle. He went out the back door and down to the shed, the wooden walkway between the big pine and the cabin wall groaning beneath his feet. He heard the song of the creek.

There was a scratching sound. A chipmunk poked his head around the pine about six feet up, then chattered at his intrusion. The shed door lock was stiff. It needed some WD-40. Inside it was dark. He felt for the switch. The forty-watt bulb on the wire cast shadows, the stacked pile of split pine and fir lent its smell.

Hanging on nails on the wall were an old bow saw, some ancient spinning rods and an old wicker creel. Some trolling rigs with golden spinners dangled next to them. Three old yellow wicker deck chairs were piled up in the back corner. He remembered when he and his cousin had spray-painted them for his aunt. The ax with the red handle stood against the wall, right where he left it the last time he was here.

He piled some wood in his arms and went back into the cabin. The basket by the fireplace had paper, kindling and matches and soon he had a bright fire going. He went out to the van and grabbed the bags of groceries from the back. Milk, butter, bread, hamburger, noodles, a six-pack of Miller's, coffee, a quart of half and half, bacon and eggs and a box of cereal. He brought them inside, into the kitchen. The old Amana door creaked as he swung it open, and he turned the knob up to get the compressor going. The small sink, the knotty pine cupboards, the radio on the windowsill, everything was right.

He made another trip to the van and got his laptop and his travel bag. A car went by, headed for Valli's maybe. The headlights bounced off the pines in front of the cabin and he could see the 'Knee-me' mailbox with the trout on top out by the road. He breathed in the pine air, his head clearing from the long drive. He went inside. The screen door banged shut behind him.

After he put his clothes in the bedroom, he sat down in his uncle's chair in the corner of the living room by the picture window and turned on the lamp. Warm light flooded the area outside by the deck, and he could just see the creek pouring down over the rocks in the circle of light. The bronze dippy bird looked at him from the stand by the couch against the far wall. The fire took the chill off, the room warmed. He opened the laptop and turned it on. The startup tone sounded foreign, out of place in the room.

He awoke around one a.m. Sometime while he was writing, he had set the laptop on the end table and fallen asleep. The once-roaring fire was down to embers, and the red-hot coals cast dancing shadows on the knotty-pine walls. The room was peaceful, a quiet presence. He stood up and stretched. He went in the kitchen and looked in the far left cupboard. Back in the corner on the top shelf was a bottle of vodka, half-full. He grinned to himself. Some things never change.

He pulled it out and got a water glass, poured himself a stiff shot. Drank it down. He could feel the heat start in his stomach and move outward. His publisher wanted five chapters by the end of the week. Maybe he'd get them done, maybe not.

He poured another shot, chugged it, and then went in the bathroom and brushed his teeth. The alcohol numbed his senses, and he didn't think about things, about his unfinished book or his uncle dying. He was here, and it was a sanctuary. He pulled off his pants and shirt and crawled into bed. Dreamless sleep.

Hot sun through the window awakened him, warming his back. He felt both refreshed and empty. For a moment he thought he heard his aunt stirring in the kitchen, an audible memory. He was wrong.

He sat up and put his head down between his knees. The comforter smelled of saddles and shoes. But everything about his aunt smelled that way. He swung his legs over and headed for the john. When he came out, he pulled on his jeans and an old red and blue ski sweater. There was a chill in the house, a good chill. Coffee, heavy on the cream, Cheerios also heavy on the cream, like his aunt taught him, the radio playing Hank Williams and then Michael Peterson. Old and new. It was right.

The new rod was in the back of the van, next to the silver case. In the case was the old Pflueger rod, the one his uncle gave him. He took it out.

I'll use this one today.

He put the sections together, the old bamboo slipping into the ferrules like lovers, and flexed the rod. It was still limber, the brown wood flashing in the sunlight. He pulled out the red box with the Medalist 1494 reel in it. He had fastened a new tippet and leader to the same green line he had been using for 30 years. Years in the water had cracked the line in places, but it still floated and ran through the guides with a whispering song. He put the reel on the rod and pulled the line through the guides. Fished in the pocket of his vest for one of the new Niemi Specials he'd ordered from the Joseph Fly Shoppe. He had about ten of the originals left, but he didn't use them. He slipped the tippet through the eye and twisted the fly around until the line wrapped tight against itself.

Then he took the long end, pushed it through the loop by the eye, and pulled it tight. He put the fly up close to his eye to make sure it was right and then bit off the excess line. Then he drew back the rod and gave the fly a couple of whips.

It was like opening a box of memories. Many fish, many rivers, days of heat and cold, rough water, smooth green, caddis flies hatching in the canyon in June, leaking waders half full of water, a swig from the little silver flask of Blue Mountain Mule Kick, the sun going down over Chief Joseph Mountain, thunderclouds above the Lostine.

He laid the rod down in the back of the van, checked his tackle box and vest, and then went back to the cabin. He locked the door and patted the screen.

"I'll be back when I catch my limit."

He climbed into the van, backed it around and drove down the pine needle driveway to the road. Turn right, no one coming, head toward Joseph. The valley was green between Joseph and Enterprise, up over the ridge where you can see the long wall of the Wallowas and then down into the little valley, headed for Lostine. Through town, the old stone tavern empty, the house with all the cars still cluttering the side of the road, fifteen miles into Wallowa.

The purple church, still vacant, sat with empty eyes on the main street. Ten years before, some locals made it into an antique gallery, but now it was for sale again. He remembered he used to talk about starting a church there with his wife, but then they drove on and he never did.

In the canyon, it was cool, an Oregon fall day. He drove to the turnout and pulled across the road into it, facing down the river. He opened the side door and sat down, pulled on his waders and went through the pockets of his vest once more. Mucilin, extra flies, leaders, filleting knife in the leather holster, trout bag, net.

He got out the rod and hefted it. It felt good, real in his hand. Not empty like the rod he bought at the sport shop. It had life; it had...

He scrambled down the bank and stepped into the water. It was late in the year, water low, lots of rocks sticking out with the once slippery green moss now dried to a dusty grey-brown. He pushed out into the water, felt the coolness through the boots. He cast out into mid-stream, the fly landing in the riffle and carrying down the current. Nothing. Another cast. A silver flash and a tug, but it was tiny. He pulled the struggling trout in, wet his hand and picked it up. The fly was as big as its mouth. He gently removed it. A little blood, not much, put it in the water. It streaked for the far shore and disappeared under the bank.

He moved on down the river. Trying in the middle, on the sides. He stood at the head of a riffle and let the fly run into the deep pool under the tree. He felt the familiar tug. An explosion of water and the fish cleared the surface. Not huge, but a keeper—eight, maybe nine inches. Brought it in, netted it. Into the trout bag. He remembered filling his bamboo creel with ten trout over ten inches in two hours, but that was a long time ago. They didn't make creels like that anymore, anyway.

He worked his way down the bank close to the road. A strike, but the fish jumped and spit out the fly.

The river came to a bend and split around an island in the middle. He waded out stood on the gravel drift. He closed his eyes and remembered.

In the right branch of the split, a big aspen had fallen into the river. The tree lay across from the near bank to the island; the water poured under it. There was a big hole close to the current where the roots had pulled out, filled with still water. He reeled in his fly until he could grab it and worked his way across, bracing against the trunk, holding the line in his left hand. When he got to the bank, he was on the other side of the fallen tree from the big hole. He had maybe four feet of line out, the fly in his hand. On a whim, he dropped it over the log onto the surface of the pool.

He saw the fish coming from the bottom of the pool straight at the fly. It was huge and hungry. Mouth wide open, the big trout barely broke the surface as it nosed over and carried the fly down toward the bottom. Without thinking, he jerked the rod up. The fish hit the end of the line. The rod bent almost in half. He released the lock on the reel and the line sang as it headed toward the middle of the river.

A vee wake followed the line, cutting through the water. He scrambled up on the log and moved the tip around a branch to keep the line from snagging. He almost lost his balance and fell, but he caught himself. The lunker headed downstream, and he brought the tip up—slowly this time, the rod bent again, but he pulled the tip around and brought the fish sideways to the rod to take the pressure off.

A gout of water exploded in midstream as the fish leaped and twisted. The effort carried the fish at least two feet into the air and it jerked its head, trying to spit the fly. Down it went, and it headed for the far bank, but he pulled its head up and cranked the reel, bringing it around. It ran again, heading for the opposite bank, but again he led it back, cranking in more line.

Again and again the fish bolted for freedom, and each time he pulled the tip up and cranked in more of the line until the great fish was only five feet away. He worked his way down the log until he could step down onto the bank. The fallen tree was still between him and the trout, so he edged around the hole in the bank, lifting the line over the root ball.

Now the fish was in front of him, still running along the bottom. He moved to the right where there was a sandy bank. He reeled the fish in until it was close enough to lift out. As he lifted it out of the water there was a sharp crack and the top section of the pole bent down. With a convulsive jerk the fish dropped on the sand and lay there, its gills working as it tried to get oxygen.

He stared at the rod. It wasn't a clean break; it had splintered.

He pulled out his pocketknife and cut the fish loose. He held the rod in his hands. The fish gave a few more jerks on the sand. He looked at the fish and then he pushed it with his toe back into the water. The fly was still in its mouth. It floated there for a moment, letting the water flush its gills. Then, in a flash, it was gone.

He picked up the rod and walked up the bank to the road.

8

ANEROID

He started the trip to Aneroid Lake early in the morning from the cabin. He took his Pflueger fly rod out of the silver case. He looked at the cracked tip and smiled.

He would have loved that I broke it on the biggest fish I ever caught in the canyon.

He had to go back to Walla Walla to see his aunt. He would take it to Ernie's shop. Ernie could fix anything.

He strapped the new rod to his daypack. He wore the old red and blue ski sweater over a tee and his old jeans.

Six miles. Should take two hours.

He went back and locked the cabin and hid the key under the stump. He patted the screen door as he went by.

I'll be back when I get my limit.

AS HE WALKED, HE REMEMBERED ANOTHER BROKEN ROD. Another day they hiked to Aneroid a million years ago, before his uncle got sick and could walk anywhere in the high mountains. They started early. Coffee. Bowls of cheerios with half and half. Two sandwiches from the refrigerator. Rods, creels, jackets with the sandwiches now in the zipper pouch. Up past the pump house, take the trail to the left. Cross the river.

For the first couple of miles, they climbed a series of steep, dusty switchbacks. Rocks in the trail, mounds of horse poop, pines rising above, shading the path. An empty plastic water bottle caught his uncle's attention.

"Idiots." He watched as his uncle flattened the bottle, rolled it up and stuck it in his jacket.

"Pack it in…" His uncle grinned. The sun flashed gold.

The litany of the wilderness. Like sitting in St. Paul's Episcopal.

Send your Holy Spirit to renew our broken hearts…

"… Lord of Love, save us and help us."

Forgive our despair, fill us with hope, and teach us to trust in your goodness…

"… Lord of Love, save us and help us."

Grant us patience with you, ourselves, and one another…

"… Lord of Love, save us and help us."

Pack it in…

"... Pack it out."

He always wondered how polite it was to tell God you were impatient with him. Today he did not need to be impatient with God because everything was right.

They came to the waterfall and then the dam. The pipe from the dam went down the hill to the powerhouse lighting the north end of the lake.

They walked on. He looked back. Wallowa Lake lay down in the deep bowl behind them, the moraine rising on the east side, bare and brown. Darkish clouds were forming out over the prairie beyond, but as he watched they moved off to the east.

Above, the sun was hot and bright. On the right side of the trail was an open slope covered in Indian Paint Brush, the red carpet a slash against the green trees. More liturgy...

... the blood of Christ...

The trail crossed a slide area, great tumbled blocks of gray granite, green grass growing among them and lightly mottled lichens turning their surface into a giant's skin.

They crossed the river again. The water-filled gorge ran up into the heart of the Eagle Cap. The trail lost its steepness. After a while they came up over a rise and the peaks appeared above the meadow. The river was smaller here, meandering down the side of the rich grass. Beaver dams turned it into a series of ponds. He could see small Brookies in the crystal-clear water.

"Too small. Another mile and we'll get the big ones."

He nodded to his uncle. The forest opened and off to the left he saw a small lake.

"Is that it?"

"Nope. That's Rogers. Aneroid is up ahead."

The trail opened ahead into a valley and Aneroid Lake came into view. They walked past some cabins. The sign said private.

"Silvertip," his uncle said.

"What?"

"Silvertip. He came up here in 1897 with tuberculosis, and the mountains made him well. He ran a pack station and built some cabins he rented out. He died at one hundred and four. This little piece is one of the few private spots in the mountains. There's another up the Lostine."

They kept walking around the lake. They came to a swampy area with tall reeds. His uncle pointed.

"You go around that side. I'll fish here. The Brookies are right out in front there along the edge of the marsh. You gotta get out into the lake without waders. It's cold." His uncle grinned.

He walked around to the other side and put the reel on his rod, rigged the line, tied on a Niemi. He stepped into the water and let the shock run up his legs for a minute. When he was used to it he waded quietly out. Out about twenty feet, the Brookies were rising. Small flies were flitting around and when they settled on the surface, the hungry fish snapped them up. He cast out. The fly sat there for a moment, and then the surface of the water broke as a big trout rushed the fly. He tried to set the hook too soon, and the trout escaped, but the fly snapped back into the reeds.

He gave a tug. It wouldn't come out. He jerked it hard three times, and he heard a crack. He looked up. The tip of his rod pointed at an awkward angle toward the reeds.

Oh no!

He pushed into the reeds, but they were too thick, so he got his pocketknife out and cut the line. Then he waded back to the shore and looked at the tip of his rod. He had cracked it good, but it was still in one piece. He walked around to the other side where his uncle was fishing.

His uncle looked up and saw the broken tip right away. He came back to the bank, put his rod down and took the broken one. He looked it over, then looked up, a question.

"I caught the fly in the reeds. I thought it would come out."

"Pulled too hard?"

He nodded.

His uncle looked it over again. "We'll take it to Ernie. Should be an easy fix."

His uncle saw the downcast look. "Long hike for nothin'." The smile wasn't a lecture, but it was an education.

HE DROVE UP TO ERNIE'S TACKLE SHOP, GOT OUT THE silver case and went inside. The young man behind the counter looked up.

He took out the rod and showed the kid the tip. "I was hoping Ernie could fix this."

The young man shook his head. "Ernie doesn't own the shop anymore. He retired. He's in a nursing home and he doesn't remember much about anything, much less fixing fishing poles." The kid behind the counter laughed at his remark like it was a joke.

He stared at the young man.

What's funny about that? Jerk.

"Can you fix it?"

The kid shook his head. "Nope. I just sell stuff. Maybe you can get that part from the dealer."

"This rod is fifty years old. It's an antique. They don't make them anymore."

The kid shrugged. "Can't help you. Try Google."

He put the rod back in the case and walked toward the door. He stopped there. Then he turned back to the grinning young man. "This isn't a fishing pole. It's a fly rod. A Pflueger Medalist. It's older than you are by about thirty years. A fishing pole is what Huckleberry Finn used to catch catfish."

He walked out.

He thought about the big trout and wondered if it was worth it.

9

THE ROLL CAST

They were out playing at the new golf course in Richland, Washington, twenty miles from the old Hanford atomic plant. On that day, the plant released a cloud of plutonium waste into the air unannounced. It drifted downwind. They were in its path. A few months later, my uncle and his three friends all came down with a rare form of childhood leukemia. He fought it for seventeen years, but finally, it killed him.

He used to go down to Portland once every two or three months to get a blood transfusion. My aunt drove him and they would stay over at Cannon Beach for a few days while he recovered. He used to laugh about it.

"I got all brand-new blood. It was good stuff. I got so worked up I chased this pretty nurse down the hall. I caught her, too."

"What happened?"

"Well, I'm so old I forgot what to do next."

Leukemia didn't stop him. He was an outstanding golfer. He taught me to play when I was twelve. The last time we played, he was seventy-six. I was thirty-seven. I could hit the ball two hundred and seventy-five yards, but I was all over the golf course. By then he could only hit it one hundred and twenty, but his drives were straight as a pin down the middle of the fairway. We played eighteen holes. He beat me by two strokes.

The last time we fished together was two years before he died. We went down below the dam at Wallowa Lake. It was still open then. When we popped open the back of the Nomad, he handed me a coil of rope.

"What's that for?"

"I can't get down the trail any more. You can lower me down with this."

We walked across the grass and down the trail to the spillway. I fastened the rope under his arms and he walked backward down the slope. He was as light as a feather. He got to the bottom, and I climbed down after him. We stashed the rope under some bushes and started down the trail.

"I can't get out in the river anymore, so I'm going on down to the hole, do some casting. Work your way down, take your time. And bring some fish when you come."

I watched him walk away, his red fishing jacket a

flame among the overhanging brush. He was bent over, and I knew for the first time that he was old, tired. I had never seen that before.

I climbed into the river and worked my way along the side, casting into riffles and behind rocks. Pulled out a few.

It was a lovely day, I remember. Green trees and brush shaded the small canyon where the river flowed. The pine trees were farther up the hill. I didn't wear waders, and the water was cold against my legs, clear.

It was every day I ever spent on the river. It was all the fish, all the green mossy rocks, all the careful steps through deep, powerful water. It was the day my brother fell into a hole in the river and his waders filled up and he would have drowned except his friend pulled him out.

It was tearing down the Minam grade in the Chevy Nomad and seeing the canyon again. Swinging around the wide bend in the road after a day's fishing and watching the valley open before me, the green fields stretching away toward Idaho and the mountains rising straight up to nine thousand feet. Putting my hand into the icy water from Cold Springs where it flowed down into the Lostine River and coming out numb.

It was riding horseback up eight miles of switchback and coming over the top into the Frances Lake basin. Hiking down the West Side of the lake to the Harris cabin after dark, the lights from the windows making pools of light out on the water. Swimming at the marina, eating at Valli's, reading about Chief Joseph in front of the fire. Sitting out on the deck at the cabin listening to Aneroid Creek singing.

Yes, it was every day I spent on the river, and I look back and they are a tapestry, threads here and patterns there, pieces, all woven together so that one day has no edges and flows into the next, and I can still see and taste and smell them all.

I worked my way down to the pool and my uncle was there, the Dean of Blue Mountain Fly Fishermen. He was casting. He looked up and grinned. "Get any?"

The fisherman's question.

I opened my creel and showed him. He nodded. "Good, good. Did I ever show you this?"

"What?"

"It's called a roll cast. You use it when you can't raise your rod up because there are trees or brush above you. You keep the line on the surface and roll it up and over."

He showed me. The line was lying out on the water and he took the rod back and swung it forward. The line formed a perfect circle as it rolled, came over the top, and the fly landed back where it had been.

"Only one problem, the fly is wet, so it doesn't look alive. So I figured out a little trick."

He did the roll cast again, but this time as it was coming over the top he moved his hand forward and back and put a small bulge in the line. The bulge ran out to the end and just as the fly came down, it hit that rolling bulge and popped like cracking a whip. The wet flew off, and the wings fluffed. It floated down like a hopper falling off a branch and WHAM! A big trout gobbled it up. My uncle laughed. He brought the fish in, unhooked it and turned it loose.

"Show me that again."

He turned to the right and pointed to a big rock at the head of the pool. He cast out on the downside of the rock to get the line out, then once again he rolled that fly right behind that rock, cracking it dry just before it hit. WHAM! Another one. He laughed again.

I've tried for thirty-seven years to figure out how he did it. He showed me again that day and I tried, but I couldn't get it. I tried for a long time. Then it was dark, and we had to go. We went back up the trail and I hauled him up to the top. He was out of breath when I got him up, and he had to stand for a long time to catch it.

"Damn leukemia," he said, and that was all. We went back to the cabin and drove home the next morning.

I CAME TO SEE HIM ONE MORE TIME BEFORE HE DIED. I WAS living in California but when I heard he was very sick, I made the trip to Walla Walla. He was at home. My step-mother, who was a nurse, was taking care of him. He had a hospital bed in the front room and when he was up, he just wore his robe and some old slippers. I got there and before he greeted me, he went into his room and brought out a box. He gave it to me. I opened it. It was a brand new fishing jacket, top drawer. He urged me with a nod and I slipped it on. He smiled and patted me on the shoulder. His love was awkward, a tear in his eye. Two months later he died. That was thirty-six years ago, and I still have the vest. I don't wear it, I just have it. I keep it in the old kit bag he left me with the two 1494 Pflueger Medalist reels. They are in the garage next to the Pflueger Medalist fly rod in the silver case. The one with the broken tip.

SOME DAYS I JUST WISH I COULD SEE HIM AGAIN, WAITING on the front porch of the cabin, his old hat with some flies in the band, the glint of his gold bridgework as he grins. I walk up from the river and he pats me on the shoulder and I hear him say it once more.

"Get any?"

10

UP THE LOSTINE—TO THE END

They pulled up to the campsite around three. They had driven way up the canyon, following the Lostine River into the heart of the mountains. The washboard road made him drive the van slowly, and it took a while to get up to the river. When they came up on top they pulled into a turnoff that looked down at the most beautiful trout stream in America.

"It's wonderful," she said.

They had been married in January, and he brought her to the Wallowas that next summer. They had been once before, for a guided overnight pack trip into Frances Lake, before they were married. His aunt had given it to him as a gift when he graduated Bible College, but they didn't stop anywhere or fish until they got up to Frances.

The three of them rode horseback and his aunt told him about the flash flood that had trapped her and his uncle up the Lostine for two days.

His wife loved the mountains. They had never camped together for a week and she was excited. She had her own tent and camping gear when he married her. Bonus special. But she had never camped the Wallowas, except for that one night at Frances.

Coming over from Elgin that morning they stopped in the Wallowa canyon at the turnout and he showed her how to fly fish. She was a natural. He left her in a flat spot and moved downstream. They were casting for a few minutes when he heard her yell. He turned. She had a trout on. She lifted the tip of the rod to show him and the fish came out of the water.

He lifted his hand to stop her, but the fish used the tension on the line and flipped right off into the river. He laughed at the look on her face. He waded over and tapped her net.

“In here first. Then show me.” He grinned. He wondered if his bridgework flashed in the sunlight.

They fished for another hour, then headed into the valley. He glanced over at her face when they came out of the canyon and she could see the mountains marching down the west side of the valley. Her mouth was open in wonder.

They drove into the town of Wallowa, and he noticed

that the sign didn't say twenty miles an hour anymore, and there were no sheriffs parked in front of the high school. People were doing thirty. He shook his head.

"Couldn't drive through this town that fast when I was a kid." More cars passed him going thirty.

He went twenty anyway.

Another ten miles and they were in Lostine. The stone tavern was closed, but there was a band advertised for Friday night. They turned right off the highway and started into the Lostine canyon. They drove down the valley, made the big swooping right turn, and then left into the steep-walled part of the canyon. Forest on the left with barbed-wire fence and private property signs. Houses, mostly log cabins with neat yards and some gardens on the right.

The van bumped off the paved road, and they were into gravel. Another four miles and they crossed the bridge over the river. There was a switchback turn and then they hit hardpan washboard and headed up the grade. Slow going after that, but no one was on the road.

He'd been coming up here since he was twelve. Now he was forty, and it was the same. The river canyon fell away to the right, and it was a long way down to the river. They passed a few campgrounds, but he knew it was a long walk down from there to the river and longer to come back up, so he kept going. He wanted to camp right on the river.

When they got up to the top, they found the perfect campsite. A flat spot, right on a bend in the river. They started setting up, and he noticed that the sun was going down over the steep western side of the canyon. It was only 4:00 in the middle of the summer. He looked up at the canyon and realized for the first time that it ran north and south. By the time they finished and got a fire going, it was nearly dark. They ate by the light of the campfire and the darkness closed in around them.

"I didn't know it got this dark in here," he said. She looked around and nodded. When they went to bed the fire had died down and he could see nothing beyond the fire ring.

He had to get up in the night. It was pitch black. He couldn't see his hand in front of his face. The darkness was almost oppressive. He fumbled for a flashlight and stumbled outside to find the toilet. The light seemed to be beaten back by the darkness. He looked up and in the narrow slit of sky between the steep walls of the canyon he could see some stars. But they did nothing to light the forest.

In the morning they had breakfast in the half-light. The sun didn't come over the eastern canyon wall until almost 11:00.

"It's too dark in here," he said. She nodded in grateful agreement.

"Let's find a canyon that runs the other way."

They broke down the tent and packed up. He remembered coming up there when he was twelve, and then he remembered that they never stayed. Always in early and out early. Now he knew why.

They drove back down the canyon. A few cars passed them going up. They stopped at a turnout and took pictures of the river. It really was beautiful. The water was crystal clear, running over gravel beds that turned into stretches of rocky bottom. Where the river made a turn, there were sand beaches. Here and there were piles of drift logs along the shore, and he knew that trout lurked in the dark shadows.

"I'd love to fish here, but it'll take a while to get where we are going."

They went up to Joseph and out to the Imnaha. They turned right at Ollokot campground and went up the gravel road to Indian Canyon Campground. It was spotless and clean, with running water and vault toilets. The canyon ran east and west. The sun woke them early and stayed with them all day. They waded in the river and he fished every morning. It was good. As good as it gets.

THEY WENT BACK TO THE WALLOWAS EVERY YEAR FOR thirty years. After a while they stopped tent camping and got a trailer. They found a nice RV campground with full service and showers. It was hard getting old, but they still went. And every time they went, they took a day trip up the Lostine. They remembered the darkness and planned accordingly. The last time they went, the world had changed. People had been told they had to stay at home. The only alternative was to go camping. So when they got up to Two-Pan trailhead at the top of the Lostine canyon, they found three hundred cars parked along the road—people walking around at seven thousand feet altitude wearing surgical masks and looking for a signal on their smartphone, trashing the campgrounds, leaving toilet paper and human refuse unburied in the woods and fire rings filled with unburnable garbage. Cars roaring up and down the road like it was Daytona.

He drove back with a broken heart. The beauty was gone. People who did not understand what to do in the wilderness filled the woods. They had forgotten the liturgy.

He thought of his uncle, what he would say, and then he was glad his uncle was gone. They drove home to Idaho. He wanted people to know; he wanted people to remember.

He wanted them to see the sun going down over Chief Joseph Mountain and the little breeze that sprang up and shattered the surface of the lake into a million diamond fragments. He wanted them to feel the tug of a big trout that found your worm in the darkness forty feet down. He wanted them to hear the wind in the pine tops, to breathe air that was clean, to see the green grass of the prairie pushing its way right to the base of Mount Howard. He wanted them to know the safety of someone who stands beside you and shows you how to cast into a green sliding river. The rush when a fourteen-incher takes the fly and runs. He wanted to show them the roll cast.

But even as he wrote it down, he knew that those days had vanished. Like Pautzke's Golden Nuggets, like Walter Brennan, like his uncle. He shrugged as he wrote the last words. Maybe someone would understand.

He put the title at the top of the manuscript and turned off the computer.

EPILOGUE

Now that I've written it, I realize that this book was more than just a lamenting of the sad state of our disappearing wilderness. As each story came to me I saw that most of them, if they involved my love for the wilderness and the river, also involved my relationship with my uncle. This morning when I got up I remembered something very important about his life, so I will speak to it in this little epilogue.

My uncle Fred came to Walla Walla in the early 1930s from Eugene, Oregon to set up his office. It was the heart of the Great Depression. He was a founding partner in a CPA firm in Walla Walla that at one time was one of the largest in the Pacific Northwest. My aunt told me that back when he started he often worked for people who sometimes could only afford to pay him with a chicken or some vegetables, but he never turned them down and many of those early clients, if they survived the rigors of those difficult economic times, became the leading citizens of our town, and lifelong friends.

He had a passion. He was an investor, not in the stock market, but in lives. He had hundreds of clients. He not only did their taxes but he was involved with them as friend, golf partner and fishing buddy.

Local ranchers and businessmen came to him over the years and asked him to help them make a plan for their wealth after they died. In Walla Walla there are several buildings on the Whitman College campus, including the Theater and the Science building that came about because my uncle suggested a large donation to the college to relieve tax burdens on heirs.

He loved investing in young people. I was one beneficiary of that passion, but there are many others who can look back and remember. He brought many young men on board in his company who later became successful CPAs and accountants in their own right. And one way he poured into their lives was to take them fishing. The cabin became a hub for young men who were learning the ropes and, though he was careful about their education, he did not spare them from solid life lessons.

Once when he had a group of partners from his office up for a fishing trip, he brought along one of the new junior partners. They went up the Lostine River to fish.

Before they split up Uncle Fred gave them the rules—the one who catches the least number of fish cleans *all* the fish. When they met up a few hours later, the first guy had six, the second, seven, and the junior partner had three. He looked at my uncle and Fred handed him his creel. It was so heavy the youngster almost dropped it. So he set about to clean the fish.

He cleaned the six, he cleaned the seven, he cleaned his and then he opened my uncle's creel. There were two fish inside and, covered by leaves, a very large rock . The lesson learned was priceless and timeless. Always look before you leap.

When he died, I was in Bible College. My aunt called me.

"Isn't there a scripture about fishing in the Bible?" she asked.

"Yes, there is," and I gave her Matthew 4:19:

> "Then He said to them, Follow Me, and I will make you fishers of men."

To me, it was perfect.

A FEW YEARS AGO I WENT WITH MY WIFE TO DAYTON, Washington, the little town outside Walla Walla where both sides of my family homesteaded and farmed, starting in the late 1800s. We went to visit the graves of my aunt and uncle in the Dayton City Cemetery. We looked all around, but I was having difficulty finding the spot where they were buried. A fellow drove by in a golf cart. He obviously worked there, so I stopped him and asked him where the graves were. He had a book with the layout of the cemetery, and he directed us to the spot.

We found the graves. They had both been such a force in my life, and I must confess I shed some tears. As I stood there, I realized that next to my aunt was the grave of Alice Nicholson Patrick, my great-grandmother. She was the daughter of D. W. Nicholson, who was the Indian Agent at Lapwai, Idaho, in the late 1800s. He was an honest agent, and the Nez Perce respected him. Nicholson was a miller and when he came to the Clearwater River, he built a mill on a small island. One year the river flooded and the rising water trapped the Nicholson family. The Nez Perce saw what was happening, swam their horses out to the island, and rescued them.

I looked further. The next grave was my great-uncle Edgar Patrick, the man I am named after. He was a flamboyant character who made and lost several fortunes in real estate and other ventures. A *bon vivant* and the best dresser in Walla Walla, or so they say.

There were more. John Franklin Rockhill, my mother's grandfather. He owned a ranch outside Dayton that was in our family over one hundred years. He was a Washington State Senator and son of Anthony Rockhill, who came to Columbia County from Independence, Ohio, a town only thirty miles from Apple Creek, Ohio, the setting for my first novels, though I did not know that when I wrote them.

As I raised my eyes, I could see the names of more of my family: Donahoe, Rockhill, Hopkins, Nicholson, Patrick, Craig, Niemi—they were all there, all around me. And in the center, my uncle with a picture on his gravestone of a man in a stream, fly fishing and the scripture I had chosen carved above it. "Follow me and I will make you fishers of men."

And as I stood there, it came to me. We all need roots. We all need family, and we all need someone in our lives to point the way to truth.

THESE ARE TROUBLED TIMES. THE THINGS I READ IN THE Bible tell me that this could be the end of days as we know them. And at the end of my own days I am convinced that God has given every person on this earth a chance to reconcile with Him. Oh, we all know the scriptures: "All have sinned and fallen short of the glory of God; The wages of sin is death but the gift of God is life eternal in Christ Jesus, For God so loved the world..."

And many dismiss them as just another "religion" selling its wares to gullible souls who need a crutch.

But as one who has tried all those other religions, I can tell you that the only God who ever answered my prayers is the God of Abraham, Isaac, and Jacob. I have studied the Bible in depth and I have come to the same conclusion that many skeptical men like General Lew Wallace, Lee Strobel and Josh McDowell have reached. Jesus Christ *is* the way, the truth and the life.

My uncle knew that. And so he set about to answer the question, "How then should we live?" by using his own life as an example. Tell the truth, be honest in all your dealings, serve the Lord. When he said grace at a meal, it was a simple prayer: "Bless this food to our use and us to your service." And if he is my example, then can I do any less?

So I will try to use the gift He has given me to plant seeds, set hooks and reel the lost and dying in from the dark.

And then one day when I finally say goodbye to the river, and I go to see Jesus, He'll grin and that flash of light I see might be some gold bridgework in his teeth or it might just be the glory of God.

And He'll look at me and say, "Get any?"

-30-

ABOUT THE AUTHOR

Patrick E. Craig is a lifelong writer and musician. After retiring from the ministry in 2007 he concentrated on writing and publishing fiction books. He has published six Amish novels, two YA mystery books, one World War II historical novel and two Anthologies of Amish stories. He lives in Idaho with his wife Judy.

ABOUT THE AUTHOR

ALSO BY PATRICK E. CRAIG

A Quilt For Jenna

The Road Home

Jenny's Choice

The Amish Heiress

The Amish Princess

The Mennonite Queen

The Journals of Jenny Hershberger

The Mystery of Ghost Dancer Ranch

The Lost Coast

The Amish Menorah and Other Stories

A Christmas Collection

The Gettysburg Letter - Coming in 2021

Contact Patrick at pec@patrickecraig.com

Website: https://www.patrickecraig.com

BOOKS BY PATRICK E. CRAIG AND MURRAY PURA

Far On The Ringing Plains

The Scepter and The Isle — Coming in 2021

The Amish Menorah and Other Stories

by The Men of Amish Fiction

A Christmas Collection

by the Men of Amish Fiction

Contact Patrick at pec@patrickecraig.com

Website: https://www.patrickecraig.com

www.ingramcontent.com/pod-product-compliance
Lightning Source LLC
Chambersburg PA
CBHW071539100726
47908CB00004B/1440

* 9 7 8 1 7 3 4 7 6 3 5 1 5 *